MW01040764

The Bridal Wreath Bush

Also by Kathryn Tucker Windham

The Bridal Wreath Bush

KATHRYN TUCKER WINDHAM

ILLUSTRATED BY
JOHN SOLOMON SANDRIDGE

BLACK BELT PRESS
Montgomery

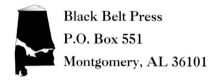
Black Belt Press
P.O. Box 551
Montgomery, AL 36101

ISBN 1-880216-92-2

First Printing

Design by Randall Williams

Printed in the United States of America

*The Black Belt, defined by its dark, rich soil, stretches across
central Alabama. It was the heart of the cotton belt. It was and is a
place of great beauty, of extreme wealth and grinding poverty, of
pain and joy. Here we take our stand, listening to the past, looking
to the future.*

To the memory of my father,

JAMES WILSON TUCKER,

who told me this story.

When I was a child, back in the late 1920s, one of my duties was to keep fresh flowers or greenery in the wall vases that hung on each side of our wide front door. One morning my father, on his way to work at the bank, saw me cutting fronds of white blossoms from the bridal wreath bush in our front yard, and he walked over to me.

"Did I ever tell you the story of that bridal wreath bush?" he asked.

"No, sir."

"You need to know about those flowers," he replied, and this is the story he told me.

When he was a younger banker, back about 1910, he had a colored customer named Hiram. Hiram owned a few acres of land out on the edge of town, and he was a good farmer. He borrowed money from the bank nearly every year at planting time to buy seeds, fertilizer, and whatever else he needed to make a crop. He always repaid his loans on time, took pride in keeping his credit good.

One day Hiram came into the bank and asked to see my father. After they had exchanged pleasantries, Hiram said, "Mr. Jim, I want to borrow twenty-five dollars, please."

It wasn't planting season and twenty-five dollars was a lot of money back then, so my father asked, "Why do you need the money, Hiram? You don't owe the bank anything now. Why do you want to go in debt again?"

Hiram hesitated before he answered. He looked down at his hat and turned it slowly by its worn brim.

"Mr. Jim," he said slowly, "I ain't never talked about this before. You know I was born in slavery up in Tennessee. I had a good master, a kind man. When I was about eighteen years old I reckon — we didn't never know for sure exactly how old we were — I fell in love with a girl over on the next plantation, a girl named Sarah. I used to slip off over there to see her. She loved me, too.

"Well, like I said, my master was a good man. When he found out about me and Sarah, 'stead of punishing me, he bought Sarah so we could get married. Even gave me a suit of clothes, and Missus gave Sarah a pretty white wedding dress. Had lace on it. We was married in the front hall up at the big house. I helped Missus gather dogwood and wild honeysuckle to decorate with.

"We was so happy, Sarah and me.

"Then my master took a notion to move to Texas. We loaded furniture and stuff in big wagons and set out. I don't know how many days we had been traveling when we got to this part of the country. We camped one night in that big grove of oak trees up on the hill above Mile Branch. You know where that is, don't you?"

My father nodded.

"Well, after supper four or five white men, men who lived around there, came and got in a poker game with my master. My master told me to light a chunk of fat pine and hold it so they could see the cards.

"My master loved to gamble. Mostly he was lucky at cards, but he wasn't lucky that night. Those men won all his money and nearly everything else he had. Finally he told them, 'I ain't got nothing left, so we'll play for Hiram. Winner take all.'

"I couldn't hardly believe it. But I stood there holding that pine torch so those men could see to gamble for me. Out in the shadows behind me I could hear Sarah sniffling. She was scared. I was, too. I watched every card that was played, and I prayed harder than I had ever prayed, but it didn't do no good.

"My master lost.

"Early the next morning, he and his family headed for Texas, taking Sarah with them. I never saw my Sarah again."

Hiram wiped his eyes on his shirt sleeve. "Long time ago. Long time ago. I still can't hardly talk about it." He wiped his eyes again and then continued. "After the War, after I got my freedom, I married again. You know my family, Mr. Jim. I got a good wife and good children. Grown children now. Can't keep up with how many grandchildren I got. But I ain't never forgot Sarah.

"Not long ago I got word that Sarah was living over in southeast Alabama, over near Enterprise. I want to go see if I can find her. I need the money to make the trip, to go look for Sarah."

"How are you going?" my father asked.

"I'm going to ride my mule."

"That's a long way to ride a mule, and you're an old man, Hiram."

"Yes, sir. I know. But I feel like I got to go try to find Sarah."

My father loaned him the money.

I don't know how long it took Hiram to make the journey or where he ate and slept along the way. As he neared Enterprise, he began asking if anyone knew an old colored woman named Sarah. Finally he found an elderly sharecropper who told him, "I believe I know who you are looking for," and gave him directions to a nearby farm.

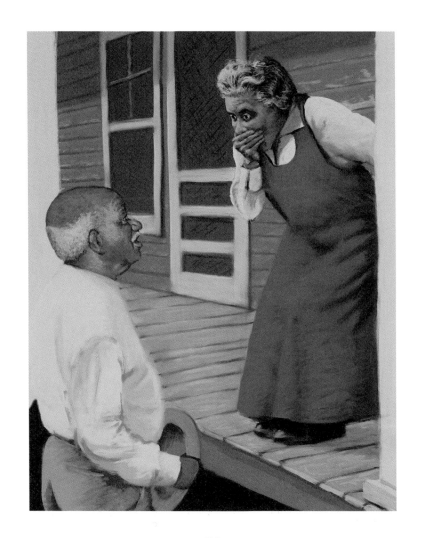

26

Hiram turned his mule off the main road down a dirt lane. At the end of the lane, a wire fence encircled a big yard, and a neat, weathered house stood in the enclosure. Even at a distance Hiram could see that the yard was bright with flowers.

He was tying his mule to a fence post when a woman walked out onto the porch. There was something familiar about the way she walked and stood.

"Sarah? Is that you?" Hiram asked.

"Is that you, Hiram?" she replied.

And so, after more than half a century, Sarah and Hiram were reunited.

*S*arah had also remarried and had reared a large family. Her husband made Hiram welcome and listened in silence as he and Sarah talked far into the night about the events that had filled their lives since the fateful poker game.

The next morning, when Hiram was saddling his mule to begin his long journey home, Sarah asked, "Hiram, who gave you the money to come over here?"

"My friend at the bank, Mr. Jim, let me have it."

"I want to send him a present," Sarah said. "See that bush over there with the white flowers all over it, that bridal wreath bush? Get a spade out from under the front steps and dig it up. Get plenty of dirt with it. I want you to take it to Mr. Jim."

Hiram dug up the bush and wrapped its roots in a croker sack. He rode all the way home holding that bush in front of his saddle.

The first thing he did when he got home was to go to the bank to see my father.

"Did you find her?" my father asked.

"Yes, sir, I did. I found Sarah. And she sent you a present." Hiram pointed to the flowering shrub he had set down outside the door.

My father didn't thank Hiram — they both knew it is bad luck to thank anyone for a growing plant. "It's mighty pretty," he said. "Let's go plant it."

They walked together across the railroad tracks, through the lumber yard and up the hill to our house where they planted the bush in our front yard.

Every spring, until I was grown and left home, I cut sprays to go in the wall vases on our porch from that bridal wreath bush — Sarah and Hiram's bridal wreath bush.

About the Story

My father, who told me many stories, told me this one when I was about nine years old. He told it only once, but I never forgot it. Even as a child I wondered what it would be like to love someone over a span of half a century, to love as deeply as Hiram loved Sarah. Now, as an old woman, I have written this story my father told me more than seven decades ago. I have written it as an affirmation that love and hope and friendship and beauty do endure.

— K. T. W.

About the Bridal Wreath Bush

Spiraea prunifolia 'plena,' also known as the bridal wreath bush, is considered the most attractive of the spring-blooming *Spiraea*. A favorite of florists, it is frequently compared to baby's breath and occassionally appears in funeral arrangements. This unusual, drought-tolerant plant needs full sun and can grow up to six feet tall under the right conditions. Originally found in China and Korea, the bush was brought to the southeastern United States before the Civil War. Almost exclusively Southern, the bridal wreath bush is common in the area from upper Tennessee to lower Alabama (zones 6, 7, and 8), and is sometimes found as far north as New York and Ohio (zones 4 and 5). The bridal wreath bush blooms in spring and stays green until winter, usually losing its leaves around mid-October.